THE DIVINE ENCOUNTER

Meeting Jesus in Eucharistic Adoration

MARK HART

Published by The Word Among Us Press
7115 Guilford Drive, Suite 100
Frederick, Maryland 21704
wau.org

27 26 25 24 23   2 3 4 5 6

ISBN: 978-1-59325-613-5
eISBN: 978-1-59325-614-2

Unless otherwise noted, Scripture texts in this work are taken from the *New American Bible, revised edition* © 2010, 1991, 1986, 1970 Confraternity of Christian Doctrine, Washington, D.C., and are used by permission of the copyright owner. All rights reserved. No part of the *New American Bible* may be reproduced in any form without permission in writing from the copyright owner.

Scripture quotations marked RSVCE are from the Revised Standard Version of the Bible—Second Catholic Edition (Ignatius Edition), copyright © 2006 National Council of the Churches of Christ in the United States of America. Used by permission. All rights reserved.

The Reverend Michael Morgan, J.D., J.C.L.
Censor Librorum
May 16, 2022
+Most Reverend Felipe J. Estévez, S.T.D.
Bishop of St. Augustine
May 17, 2022

Cover design by Suzanne Earl
Cover photograph courtesy of Life Teen International

Library of Congress Control Number: 2022908980

Dedication

To all the truly good priests—too often forgotten, misunderstood, or just plain unappreciated—I say thank you. Through your hands, our Lord is made present. Through your yeses, souls are claimed, reborn, and made new. Through your words, sins are absolved and matter confected. Through your support, couples thrive and families are encouraged to grow. Through your sacrifices, though oft unseen, countless sinners find refuge in Mother Church. And through your willingness to offer yourselves as a living sacrifice, the once-and-for-all sacrifice is made available to us all upon altars and within tabernacles the world over.

So to you, the good shepherds, who guide and protect in safe, healthy, obedient, and humble ways, I say thank you for being our spiritual fathers. Your reward will be great in heaven.

Please continue to seek holiness. Please return to Confession often. Please stay rooted in the sacraments. Our Church and our world need good and holy priests. I need you.

May Mother Mary and St. Joseph, the Terror of Demons, kneel beside you, daily, in prayer.

Table of Contents

My Introduction to Eucharistic Adoration

"We're gonna do what?" I asked with a perplexed and indignant tone.

"We're going to worship the Lord," the leader replied to my smug sixteen-year-old self.

"But we just had Mass for an hour. Now we're going to pray some more? To a trophy???" My retort was in a slightly more humble but equally confused tone.

Let's back up.

I was Catholic. Born and baptized Catholic. Big Catholic family, parochial school, years spent as an altar boy—the whole nine yards. But *this,* this worship of a big gold Catholic vessel with the bread in it—this was a stretch for me.

I had never been introduced to Adoration. That isn't to say that it was "new"—not at all. Eucharistic Adoration of our Lord in his Most Blessed Sacrament is a prayer tradition that dates back centuries, likely to twelfth- or thirteenth-century France. For hundreds of years, Catholics of all walks of life, in all corners of the globe, have come together or alone to a chapel and have fallen on their knees before the Body, Blood, Soul, and Divinity of Jesus Christ, reserved in their local tabernacles. Of course, I had no historical frame of reference nor spiritual thought about this practice one way or another.

I mean, I was sixteen years old and still trying to wrap my head around the fact that our Catholic Church teaches that the Communion bread is not merely a symbol of Jesus but, through the power of the sacramental priesthood, actually transforms (more to the point, transubstantiates) *into Christ himself.* So imagine my surprise when my youth minister explained after Mass that the priest was going to place a consecrated host into this large decorative vessel (called a "monstrance") so that we could kneel and worship what was bread just moments before but was now our Lord. It was too much to wrap my head around.

The luna (the small circular "holder" for the Eucharist) was placed in the monstrance, and the now sacred vessel was positioned atop the altar in the sanctuary. The candles flickered. The incense rose. The silence was profound and, at the same time, almost deafening. The light hit the golden casing and seemed to radiate throughout the darkened church.

The more I gazed upon the Eucharistic center, the more entranced I became. My heart felt drawn toward the Eucharist; I was able to focus my prayer in a new way. I didn't know exactly what was happening, but I was sure of two things: First, that this was not merely bread. Second, I was experiencing a deeper and more abiding peace than ever before. I was lost in the moment, in the silence, and in the space. The Lord was present, and not just in my mind.

There was some music, but I don't remember the songs. There were some prayers uttered that I didn't know. There was a blessing I faintly recall.

I exited the Church unsure of what I had just experienced but certain that upon the altar was no mere "what" but rather a "Whom." For possibly the first time in my angst-filled, stressed-out, self-consumed adolescent life, I had felt true peace outside of the confessional. The first question I asked my leader was "When are we doing this again?"

Now, I'd love to say that my every encounter in Adoration has been as soul stirring and profound as on that night over thirty years ago. But that would land me right back in the confessional. I've probably been to Adoration now hundreds if not thousands of times. Some moments have been life altering, others unforgettable for some moment of insight or intimacy the Holy Spirit granted, and still others just normal brief encounters that offered peace and strength for the daily journey.

It was in an Adoration chapel that I first felt God's true presence in my life and daily walk. It was in Adoration that I first heard the call to marry my then girlfriend, though we were only teenagers. It was in Adoration that I found solace and peace thousands of miles from home and community on any number of trips. It was in an Adoration chapel that I proposed. It was in Adoration that I said yes to ministry. It was in Adoration that my wife and I named our kids. It was in an Adoration chapel that I sought Jesus for mercy and compassion and healing during the most challenging moments of my life.

Put simply, when people ask me about my relationship with Jesus Christ as a practicing Catholic, the conversation always leads back to the sacraments, then the Mass, and ultimately the Eucharist (most often, in Adoration).

Whether you are a "seasoned vet" when it comes to Adoration or the entire concept is new to you, the reality is that the Eucharist is our greatest gift as Catholics. The opportunity to worship the Lord and adore him in his Most Blessed Sacrament is one that cannot be overstated or taken for granted. Through the Eucharist, we have an opportunity for intimacy with the Lord unlike what any other denomination can offer. We are blessed beyond measure.

But Adoration is often the best-kept secret in our Church's library of prayer practices, reserved to seemingly few times and few places around any average diocese. The good news is that there is a growing move in our twenty-first-century Church to offer Adoration more widely. And while Adoration is most often thought of as taking place before the exposed Eucharist, it can also be done before the reserved Eucharist in the tabernacle. As the faithful enter into this ancient practice with more regularity, we have the opportunity to grow closer to the Lord in a unique and profound way.

I hope this little book will help you enter more deeply into Adoration and receive the blessings the Lord has for you there.

CHAPTER ONE

Why Adoration?

Adoration of the Blessed Sacrament is a gift that has offered countless souls over the centuries—in both private and communal settings and regardless of culture, class, rank, or esteem—intimacy and companionship, comfort and security, assurance and peace. Jesus Christ is present to us in a unique and tangible way; he is accessible and available to adore.

At Mass we are transported to the upper room of Holy Thursday and to the foot of the cross on Good Friday. Christ's once-and-for-all sacrifice is made present. At Mass we consume and are consumed by the Lord's grace.

In Adoration we are afforded a different opportunity for intimacy. We can dwell in his holy presence as he enters ours. We gaze upon him as he gazes back at us. We "draw near to God," as St. James recommended, and have tangible evidence that he draws near to us (James 4:8).

While there is no form of prayer higher or greater than the Mass, Adoration offers us something a little different. The opportunity to just "sit with" the Lord, outside of the liturgy, is a chance like no other on the planet. God is available to us—fully present—in an alternative way.

In fact, the Church is so adamant that we do not "miss" this gift that she alerts us to God's unique Eucharistic presence in every chapel in every corner of the world by a visual reminder. The Eucharist (the consecrated host) is reserved in the tabernacle, which is Latin for "dwelling place" or, more specifically, "tent." Beside every tabernacle in the world burns a candle, most often encased in red. When one candle burns out, it is replaced with another. Thus a light offers an enduring reminder of Christ's perpetual presence not only among us—for he is Emmanuel, which means "God is with us" (Matthew 1:23)—but, even more specifically, in the sanctuary or chapel.

What I find amazing is that the eternal flame was not a Catholic idea. This is a tradition that hearkens all the way back to the time of Moses. The Book of Exodus tells us of God's prescription of a flame as a reminder of his dwelling among his people as they ventured into (and wandered in) the desert following their enslavement and escape from Egypt. You see, God's presence was in and with the ark of the covenant, which held the Ten Commandments, a pot of manna, and the priestly staff of Moses' brother, Aaron (see Hebrews 9:3-4). Since the ark "contained" the presence of God, his people placed it in a special tent (or tabernacle) that was flanked on all sides by God's priests. As a reminder to his people that he was indeed with them and would not abandon them, God prescribed the following:

> And you shall command the sons of Israel that they bring to you pure beaten olive oil for the light, that a lamp may be set up to burn continually. In the tent of meeting, outside the veil . . . , Aaron and his sons shall tend it from evening to morning before the LORD. It shall be a statute for ever to be observed throughout their generations by the sons of Isreal. (Exodus 27:20-21, RSVCE)

Isn't that amazing? God "dreamt up," well over three thousand years ago, that little red candle that alerts us to Christ's true presence in our churches. Which begs the question, why did God feel it would be necessary to remind his people of his presence? Quite simply, because he knows people better than we know ourselves, and he must have known they would need reminding!

Life gets busy. Sin distracts us. We are fallen and human and oftentimes self-focused. God loves us enough to call us out of ourselves and put a constant reminder, burning in our parishes, that we might seek and invite the Lord to burn (again) in our hearts!

> The Eucharist is the bread that gives strength. It is at once the most eloquent proof of His love and the most powerful means of fostering His love in us. He gives Himself every day so that our hearts as burning coals may set afire the hearts of the faithful.
> —**St. Damien of Molokai**

Give the Holy Spirit permission to open the eyes of your heart to the great gift of adoring the Eucharist. Ask him to reveal himself and his love in a new way while you are in his sacred presence.

CHAPTER TWO

God Desires Intimacy with Us

"Wait until your father gets home," my mother said with a bone-chilling intensity.

Far from a warm reminder of anticipation and jubilation, it was a stern warning laced with threat and impending doom. Never mind the sin and hijinks that had preceded her admonishment; her tone was clear and prophetic: my brothers and I had crossed the proverbial line in the sand, and there would be consequences.

Indeed my father did return home that night. He was a hardworking and at times quite stern man, a strong provider with an even stronger expectation of parental respect and obedience to the rules. He could be warm, sure, but oftentimes when he drew near, it signaled that a wrong needed to be made right: we had disrespected our mother or home or belongings, and we would be taught a lesson.

On this fateful night, my father scaled the stairs to our room and approached me and my fellow culprit (and older brother). He stared into our shame-filled eyes. Our lips quivering, we prepared for the worst. He then sat down beside us on the bed and—in what I can only describe as an unexpected, God-given moment of mercy—proceeded to tell us that, while he was disappointed in how we had conducted ourselves, he knew it was not our intent. We received a stern warning and a just punishment, but in retrospect, our "sentence" was lenient and filled with paternal mercy.

I often reflect on that night (and the dozens that did not end so joyfully). The experiences we have as children, good and bad, obviously and understandably shape not only our adolescent years but also our adult years and our own parenthood. Many of us can readily see how we are (and are not) like our earthly parents, for better or worse. That said, however, unless we proactively pray about it, we might fail to see how our perceptions (or misperceptions) of our earthly parents play into and influence how we view and approach our Father in heaven.

Many of us view God the Father as the "Old Testament" God, filled with fury and wrath, smiting people with the turn of every ancient page of Scripture. He's less the father in the family room than the judge in the courtroom, the one who doles out sentences that you must respect and certainly the one you do not want to cross. There's a reason they cite "fear of the Lord" as a gift of the Holy Spirit. God the Father can seem reactionary and unapproachable, a distant and inaccessible "provider" with a firm hand and high expectations of obedience and virtue.

> The Holy Eucharist is the perfect expression of the love of Jesus Christ for man, since it is the quintessence of all the mysteries of his life. I can no longer live without Jesus.
>
> **—St. Maria Goretti**

That was certainly my parochial-school perception of God the Father. Know your commandments. Follow the rules. Go to Mass. Say your prayers. Avoid hell. God was to be feared; he was often spoken about but rarely spoken to.

But I came across a verse that flips the narrative of "angry Old Testament God" right on its head:

> And they heard the sound of the LORD God walking in the garden in the cool of the day, and the man and his wife hid themselves from the presence of the LORD God among the trees of the garden. (Genesis 3:8, RSVCE)

Immediately before this scene, sin comes so the Garden of Eden. The serpent enters the picture. Adam and Eve choose themselves and abandon the God who has literally given them paradise. The fruit juice is still running down their faces when we stumble upon the verse above.

One of the details we often miss is that God was walking in the garden. Did you catch that? He was not a distant, cosmic, unapproachable God who had breathed the cosmos and spun the world into existence from some faraway and inaccessible place. No, he was so close to them that they could literally hear him taking an evening

> When I am before the Blessed Sacrament I feel such a lively faith that I cannot describe it. Christ in the Eucharist is almost tangible to me. To kiss his wounds continually and embrace him. When it is time for me to leave I have to tear myself away from his sacred presence.
> —St. Anthony Claret

stroll ("in the cool of the day") in the Garden of Eden. God the Father was so close that his children not only heard him walking but hid from him. The Creator drew near, and his creation was ashamed. Afraid, they played the world's first game of hide-and-seek.

The Father desired intimacy. The children desired escape.

We know well the story and how it ended. Our primordial parents were given everything and lost it all. We don't often focus on that first part. You may have read in the Bible or heard in a homily that God entered into a "covenant" with Adam and Eve, much as he did with Noah, Abraham, Moses, David, and others. Do we understand what that means?

A covenant is a total and complete gift of self. In and through a covenant, God basically says, "I am going to give you all of myself and withhold nothing." Then we are asked and invited to respond by doing the same.

Of course, our biblical ancestors all fell short on holding up their end. It wasn't until Jesus Christ came in the flesh and did what we could not do on our own—becoming the once-and-for-all, perfect, and final covenant—that we would be put back into right relationship with God. Remember Jesus' words at the Last Supper:

> Now as they were eating, Jesus took bread, and blessed, and broke it, and gave it to the disciples and said, "Take, eat; this is my body." And he took a chalice, and when he had given thanks he gave it to them, saying, "Drink of it, all of you; for this is my **blood of the covenant,** which is poured out for many for the forgiveness of sins." (Matthew 26:26-28, RSVCE, emphasis mine)

At the Last Supper—and on the cross—Jesus literally gave *everything that he was and had*. He didn't just uphold our end of the covenant but embodied and *became* the covenant. Jesus held nothing back. His enduring presence in the sacraments, most specifically the Eucharist, offers that same self-gift and reckless abandon.

Now picture the Eucharist. God makes himself not only present but also *available*—on every altar and in every tabernacle, in every language, in almost every corner of the world, simultaneously. Is God the distant Creator who spun the cosmos into existence and rules with an iron fist from a faraway land? Or is God near and intimate and present, eternally available to us?

The Eucharist is God's way of fulfilling Jesus' promise in Matthew 28:20 to be with us "always, until the end of the age." This is yet another reason Jesus Christ is Emmanuel, which means "God is with us" (1:23). God is a Father who keeps his word by giving us access to the Word, Jesus Christ. By extension, the tabernacle candle is the Father's way of saying, "I'll keep the light on for you."

God, in his infinite and perfect wisdom, had this plan from the very beginning, when he was available to the sinners in the garden. If condemnation came to us through what we ate, why wouldn't salvation come to us through heavenly bread?

We see clearly from Sacred Scripture that the Eucharist was not a "reactionary" or "last-minute" idea on God's part. It didn't just "come to Jesus" in the upper room that holy night. No, this was God's plan from the beginning: to offer intimacy, remain available and accessible, and transform his children from the inside out.

As you head to Adoration next time, ponder or journal about the following questions:

1. In what ways does God make his presence known to me?

2. How do I see God? As a loving Father? As a strict judge? As someone I can know, love, and trust?

3. How can I put myself in a position to hear God more clearly and be in deeper relationship with him?

4. How might time in Adoration improve or change any of my above responses?

> He could not have commanded anything more beneficial [than the Eucharist], for this Sacrament is the fruit of the tree of life. Anyone who receives this Sacrament with the devotion of sincere faith will never taste death.
>
> **—St. Albert the Great**

CHAPTER THREE

Making Ourselves Available to God

For centuries, St. Martha has been getting, for lack of a better term, "a pretty bad rap." You know the famous story, I'm sure, but let's revisit the scene in St. Luke's Gospel:

> Now as they went on their way, he entered a village; and a woman named Martha received him into her house. And she had a sister called Mary, who sat at the Lord's feet and listened to his teaching. But Martha was distracted with much serving; and she went to him and said, "Lord, do you not care that my sister has left me to serve alone? Tell her then to help me." But the Lord answered her, "Martha, Martha, you are anxious and troubled about many things; one thing is needful. Mary has chosen the good portion, which shall not be taken away from her." (10:38-42, RSVCE)

This story has been shared countless times in Christian circles. Homilies usually arrive at the same point: Be like Mary more than Martha. Be present to Jesus. Pray first, and serve second.

To be clear, these points are true. They are not only foundations of the spiritual life but also great reminders to us when going to Adoration. We must fight distraction (which we will deal with in the next chapter). We must focus more on listening to Jesus than merely serving him. We must be present to the God who is present to us.

All these things are true. That said, can we give St. Martha (ironically, the patron saint of food servers) a break, please? What was her greatest recorded crime? She was so passionate about the Lord that she sought to serve him, to be hospitable, to make him comfortable and wait on him hand and foot. If only the world had more people with Martha's heart.

I've met plenty of people who didn't love God enough; I've never met anyone who loved God too much. Still, while Martha's heart was pure and her work ethic praiseworthy, the Holy Spirit reminds us here that prayer must precede service, even service in his name.

Many of you reading this likely go to Adoration already. You are involved at your parish on different levels: serving in ministry, attending Sunday and even daily Mass, and taking part in an array of other spiritual activities. If that's the case, you might be thinking, "Why is he telling *me* this? I already know this!" But if you are the type who is always giving in the Lord's name, it might be the case that you are "a Martha," whether you know it or not.

When it comes to faith and ministry, it's oftentimes easier to serve than to be served. If we are not first fed spiritually, however, it's not really Christ we are offering others; it's ourselves. This is why God commands all of us—prayer warriors and prayer novices—-to keep holy the Sabbath.

Think about that for a minute. One of the Ten **Commandments** is *to rest*. Out of all the things that God could put into his "top ten" of most important things to remember and to do, *rest is one of them!*

Now, why would resting have to be a commandment? Because we stink at it. We are more human *doings* than human *beings*. Time, not money, is our greatest commodity. It's also the gift we most often squander or channel in the wrong direction. We lose perspective amid our busyness.

Life has a way of getting very full and very noisy. The desert mystics and early Christian Fathers often pointed to noise and speed as two great detriments to their prayer and spiritual lives. Not much has changed. Perhaps your day is as noisy and full as mine is, from the time you wake up until your head hits the pillow.

> We must not separate our lives from the Eucharist. The moment we do so, something shatters.
> —St. Teresa of Calcutta

So the question becomes, how do we downshift mentally and emotionally? How do we spiritually exhale and take full advantage of our time in Adoration? Taking fifteen or thirty minutes or eventually an entire Holy Hour to sit with the Lord is already a victory for most of us Catholics. With full-time jobs, family responsibilities, activities, and obligations, any amount of time we carve out in our day or week is something noteworthy.

Keeping holy the Sabbath is about far more than just making it to Mass for an hour. It means entering into God and being present to him. It means being present to the family he has given you and ordering your day and, by extension, your entire week to God.

Now, let's take another step. If the Mass is the central focus of our sabbath rest and worship and the Eucharist is the central focus of the Mass, the source and summit of our faith, what does that reveal to us about the role the Eucharist can play the other 167 hours a week? How might the Eucharist reorient us, when necessary, to the heart of God when we encounter a stressful Monday or mundane Wednesday or temptation-filled Friday?

Making even little pockets of time each week to stop by the church or chapel to adore the Lord in Adoration or in the tabernacle can radically change not only the course of your week but your very life. Before you know it, Adoration will go from something reactionary—something to help you "get through the week"—to something you yearn for.

This is where Martha and Mary can collide. Make a plan (as would Martha), and commit to pulling into the nearest Catholic Church at least once a week. Then make like Martha's sister, Mary, and just sit in his presence, exhaling the stress of life. Choose the better portion. Choose Jesus Christ.

As you head to Adoration next, ponder or journal about the following questions:

1. At what time of day do I pray best? How can I create space at that time of day to be more present to God?

2. Does my current schedule demonstrate that my relationship with God is a priority? How or how not?

3. Create a pie chart showing where all your time goes. What do I see about my 168-hour week?

4. What two or three things can I reschedule or eliminate in order to make Sunday a true Sabbath?

CHAPTER FOUR

Dealing with Distractions in Adoration

I was about to go live on a television interview, via Zoom. We had tested the lighting and microphones on my end. A producer was sitting two thousand miles away, whispering in my ear through the miracle of technology. I had locked the door to my home office so that my seven-year-old would not inadvertently enter, asking for a snack or help working through a level on Super Mario Bros. I knew my content and was prepared for any question the television host was about to throw at me. Or so I thought.

"Can you set your computer to 'Do not Disturb,' please, Mark, before we get started?" the producer asked as part of her standard pre-interview protocol.

"Wait, what do you mean?" I asked, confounded as to what my computer could do.

"Oh, just slide to the top right corner, and it will reveal an option to set your computer to 'Do Not Disturb,' and you won't receive any calls or texts or updates while it's on." She added in passing, "It'll ensure that we don't get interrupted during the interview."

Little did this producer realize that she had just given me the pearl of great price.

You mean, with one action I can just silence the world and be truly present? Forget Willy Wonka? *This* was the golden ticket I'd been searching for my entire professional life! Since then, not a day has gone by that I haven't utilized that practical nugget on my laptop.

It's sadly ironic that the more wireless the world has become, the more difficult it has gotten to really "unplug." My wife, Melanie, and I have a standing joke that when we have a getaway, the first day and a half "on vacation" are spent mentally and emotionally preparing to *be on vacation.* In all honesty, it's usually day three by the time I am fully and truly present to relaxation. It takes three days to mentally downshift, sever the tether to the laptop and phone, and enter into the serenity.

Perhaps I'm not alone?

Adoration is a great gift, but it can present a challenge for those of us who are perpetually on the go. It's one thing to recognize

> The Church and the world have a great need of eucharistic worship. Jesus waits for us in this sacrament of love. Let us be generous with our time in going to meet Him in adoration.
> —Pope St. John Paul II

that Christ is truly present to us in the Eucharist (as we spoke about in chapter two), but it's quite another to be truly present *to him.* The world is increasingly noisy, and spending time in silence, motionless before the unmoved Mover and uncreated Creator, can be difficult for those immersed in creation and all the distractions that come with it.

That said, there is a difference between being physically present in the chapel and being emotionally present before the Lord. The former requires discipline and time; the latter requires an ascent of the mind and movement of the heart. There are days when I sit in my Holy Hour and it feels like 58 minutes of fighting distractions and 120 seconds of peace or bliss. I might even get frustrated with myself over how disproportionate this is. But that's when it is essential to remember that heaven isn't judging me; I am.

While I may feel like a failure because of how undisciplined or unfocused or distracted my prayer is—"Two minutes, Mark? Really? That's all you could really focus on Jesus for, two lousy minutes?"—the communion of saints is cheering me on.

It's in such moments that I wish we could see God's throne room in heaven. It's filled with saints. I like to think of my namesake and patron, the saint whose name I took at Confirmation, my favorite intercessors, and other saints to whom I have a particular devotion. They are all watching and cheering me on to sanctity. It's as if St. Mark and Pope St. John Paul II are up there giving high fives, saying, "Did you see our boy Mark today? He went two full minutes undistracted and totally focused in his prayer before the Lord. That's ninety seconds longer than yesterday! Wooo hoooo!!"

A spiritual director gave me sage advice, practical steps, and a warning about distractions in prayer, especially when in Adoration. I'll lay them out briefly here, in hopes that his insights might help someone reading this.

First, always have a journal or something in which to record things. Sometimes the things distracting us are just laundry lists of things we have to do. When we sit down in silence, they flood to the forefront of our minds. There is nothing wrong with that: life is busy, and these tasks are valid. So if you need to take the first five or ten minutes in Adoration writing out a list, from "Don't forget to pay the electric bill" to "Grab milk at the store" or "Renew that prescription for Mom," then do so. Acknowledging and moving on from these things create mental space for you to be more present.

Next, if there is a situation or relationship or dilemma that is occupying all your mental energy and distracting you from your Adoration time, offer it up to God. Simply say, "Lord Jesus, (insert situation or person here) is all I can think about or focus on right now. But I want to be present to you. So, Lord, I offer this (person or situation) up for your glory. May every thought about it glorify you and draw my heart closer to yours." You may want to repeat that prayer a few times.

Now, doing this has a twofold effect. If the distraction remains in your heart and mind, it may be something the Lord wants to speak to you about. Rather than filling your prayer time with words, ask the Lord to grant you wisdom or peace or insight. He may offer you a word or a consolation in your heart. He may offer you a new perspective or a question to ponder. Even if a resolution does not quickly come, there is often a sense of peace because you have invited the Lord into this situation and given it over to him.

On the other hand, if the feelings that overwhelm you are not of God but rather of the evil one—meant to distract you or steal your peace or divert your attention from Christ in the Eucharist—then the devil will flee. "Submit yourselves to God. Resist the devil, and he will flee from you. Draw near to God, and he will draw near to you" (James 4:7-8).

The devil will never do anything that will bring glory to God. Offering whatever is distracting you for Christ's glory upends any plans from the enemy to steal your focus from the Lord. St. Paul reminds the Romans that "when [you] want to do right, evil is at hand" (Romans 7:21). He's reminding them, and us, that the devil does not sit idly by. If you are pursuing Christ, the devil will pursue you. Make no mistake, when you make time in your schedule to pray and especially go out of your way to get to Adoration, the enemy will seek to stop you.

Now, we have nothing to fear. Christ has already won the battle. And "if God is for us, who can be against us?" (Romans 8:31).

We must remember that the devil is merely a fallen angel; he is not God's equal. We have St. Michael the archangel and the host of heaven standing by, ready to defend us and do battle on our behalf. Let us be present enough to invite them in. The St. Michael Prayer is included in the Appendix of this booklet. Pray it early and often, and rest assured that the Lord and his heavenly power are indeed with you.

Third, if you have a long list of people you regularly pray for—family, friends, people in your circle of life, people for whom you've promised to pray—that is amazing, but praying for them all can be quite time consuming. We might bring that

> You left us Yourself in the Sacrament of the Altar, and You opened wide Your mercy to us. There is no misery that could exhaust You; You have called us all to this foun-tain of love, to this spring of God's compassion.
> —St. Faustina Kowalska

list to Adoration because it is our most focused time before the Lord. At times, though, the list can become a hindrance to really hearing the Lord. We might spend all our time speaking and petitioning rather than listening and receiving. God gave us two ears and one mouth, and we ought to use them in proportion.

If you feel the need to mention every person and petition by name, perhaps you can have a list in your journal that you read at the beginning of your prayer time, entrusting all of your petitions to Jesus. Maybe just say to Jesus, "Lord, I entrust everyone I normally pray for, those I've promised to pray for, and even those I've neglected or forgotten to pray for as I should, to your divine mercy and your most sacred heart. Please be with them as I seek to be with you." Then trust that the Lord has these people covered in prayer.

One warning several spiritual directors have given me over the years is the temptation to fill my time in Adoration of the Blessed Sacrament with nonstop speaking. Placing our petitions before the Lord is good and holy and brings God joy. Any time we open our hearts and mouths and bring our needs to him, it glorifies God, to be sure. That said, we can also entrust petitions to the Lord before we get out of bed and when we are driving, sitting on the couch in our living room, or kneeling beside our bed at night. Your time in Adoration is a unique gift, a moment in the course of your day or week when you can draw near to the Lord in

> If I can give you any advice, I beg you to get closer to the Eucharist and to Jesus. We must pray to Jesus to give us that tenderness of the Eucharist.
> —St. Teresa of Calcutta

a personal way, just to adore and to listen, without the crowd at Mass or the noise and busyness of home.

As you head to Adoration next, ponder or journal about the following questions:

1. Write out James 4:7-8, and journal about what it communicates to you personally.

2. Write out Romans 7:21 and 1 Peter 5:8-9. What do these warnings from Sts. Paul and Peter communicate to you about the spiritual life and its dangers?

3. Write out Mark 6:31. What does this say to you, especially as it pertains to Adoration of Our Lord in the Blessed Sacrament?

CHAPTER FIVE

God's Not Afraid
of Your Mess

It was like a war zone. The air was hazy. Debris was strewn everywhere. A discernible stench filled the air. Only the most highly trained archaeologists and forensic experts could have sifted through the mess.

It was the bedroom of our teenage daughter.

When anyone entered, they were immediately ten inches taller due to the "clean" clothes scattered across the carpet. One can only imagine the countless treasures contained beneath the mess: the Holy Grail, the ark of the covenant, Christ's burial shroud? Who knew? The room looked like something out of a college fraternity movie following an all-campus party. And at that moment, there were a precious few hours before Grandma and Grandpa were coming over for holiday dinner.

"Baby girl, you have to clean your room now," my wife pleaded compassionately.

I was a little more direct: "Sweetheart, if that room is not spotless in one hour, you will not see your friends for a month."

Sixty minutes passed, and I entered a room so immaculate you'd have thought angels bunked there. I surveyed the floor, the top of the chest, the desk and vanity. Not a speck of dust or one article of clothing out of place.

I then turned my attention to the closet. As I approached it, my daughter quickly impeded my path. "You don't need to go in there, Daddy." "Oh, I think I do, Sweetie," fearful of what might befall me (or fall on me) when I opened that door.

The hinge creaked, and a mountain of clothes shook. My daughter had hidden four metric tons of clothing in a space made for a small human—without a forklift or a team of highly skilled engineers. I'm not sure how she'd achieved this.

> Many people nowadays say, "I wish I could see his shape, his appearance, his clothes, his sandals." Only look! You see him! You touch him! You eat him!
> —St. John Chrysostom

This efficient father—who often overpacked the family SUV for trips to the beach—was thoroughly impressed. But the disciplinarian in me—who wants to teach my daughter cleanliness, appreciation, and respect for one's space and belongings—fought back. "Sweetheart, how do you live like this? How in the world do you think this is okay?" I asked in sincere confusion and disbelief.

She said something that melted my heart. "Daddy, I know I'm a mess, and you know I'm a mess, but you know you love me, and I know you love me." She grinned, kissed my cheek, and fled the scene of the crime.

My daughter had no idea how profound she had just been nor the effect that her self-assurance (and wisdom) would have on my prayer life. She was correct. She has a thousand amazing traits and attributes; she's incredible on many levels. But cleanliness is just not her "thing." Yes, I know she's a mess.

What's worse (or better, depending on how you look at it) is that *she knows and admits* that she is a mess. More importantly, she also knows that I love her. She trusts in the love of her father, regardless of the condition of her room.

A day or two later, I was sitting in my local Adoration chapel. Weighed down by a thousand things—from work situations to financial stress to extended family drama—I was feeling really scattered and reactionary and just lacking peace. The only other worshipper in the chapel left, so it was just me and Jesus, and I began to talk to him aloud. I shared my brokenness, struggles, frustrations, and even anger with certain situations. I was annoyed by all this and asking Jesus why he had not yet intervened or given me what I needed to be peaceful in the midst of so much strife. I quoted the timeless words of St. Teresa of Avila, "If this is how you treat your friends, it's no wonder you have so few."

As my impetuous rant subsided, I was filled with guilt: guilt that I wasn't a "better" Catholic or husband or father or boss. I was upset with myself for not being more patient, more virtuous, more together. I was embarrassed before God that I wasn't holier.

It was in that moment that the Lord, in his mercy, gave me exactly what I needed. He gave me loving assurance. A peace came over my heart and flooded my soul. I gazed at the Eucharist, and I was taken back to my daughter's words just days before, as we stood beside that mountain of stuff hidden in the closet.

At that moment, the perfect prayer fell from my lips: "I know I'm a mess, and you know I'm a mess, but you know you love me, and I know you love me."

Sometimes, I think, we believe we have to have it "all together" before God, when in actuality, nothing could be further from the truth. This is a God who was born in a cave and placed in a feed box. The first guests at his birthday celebration were shabby shepherds. This is not a "Do as I say, not as I do" type of God whom we love and serve.

Our God is not afraid to get his heavenly hands dirty. Let's not forget that he formed Adam out of the clay and Eve from a rib. This is a God who worked with his hands, healed with spit, and didn't just calm the storms but tread upon them. Our God is not put off by a little work or family drama. Our Lord took flesh and entered the mess. He's not afraid of yours.

> The Eucharist is a fire which inflames us.
> —St. John Damascene

Adoration is a great time to lay it all out there before the Lord (although I do suggest checking to be sure you're alone before you do so aloud). Imagine the trust it takes to speak so transparently and plainly before the God of the universe in that tabernacle or monstrance. Entrusting your greatest and worst moments to the Lord and knowing that he will not reject you but rather will embrace you say a great deal about your relationship and your belief in his true presence. There is nothing you're feeling that he doesn't already know.

Scripture reminds us that God knows all the thoughts and movements of our hearts and that before him all is laid bare. I suggest you read these verses in the presence of the Lord:

LORD, you have probed me, you know me:
   you know when I sit and stand;
   you understand my thoughts from afar.
You sift through my travels and my rest;
   with all my ways you are familiar. (Psalm 139:1-3)

Cast all your worries upon him because he cares for you. (1 Peter 5:7)

We have come to know and to believe in the love God has for us. God is love, and whoever remains in love remains in God and God in him. In this is love brought to perfection among us, that we have confidence on the day of judgment because as he is, so are we in this world. There is no fear in love, but perfect love drives out fear because fear has to do with punishment, and so one who fears is not yet perfect in love. We love because he first loved us. (1 John 4:16-19)

> **Not to go to Communion is like someone dying of thirst beside a spring.**
> **—St. John Vianney**

I am convinced that neither death, nor life, nor angels, nor principalities, nor present things, nor future things, nor powers, nor height, nor depth, nor any other creature will be able to separate us from the love of God in Christ Jesus our Lord. (Romans 8:38-39)

The LORD, your God, is in your midst,
   a mighty savior,

Who will rejoice over you with gladness,
    and renew you in his love,
Who will sing joyfully because of you. (Zephaniah 3:17)

The eyes of the LORD are directed toward the righteous
    and his ears toward their cry. . . .
The righteous cry out, the LORD hears
    and he rescues them from all their afflictions. (Psalm 34:16, 18)

Our sharing in the Body and Blood of Christ has no other purpose than to transform us into that which we receive.
—Pope St. Leo the Great

God proves his love for us in that while we were still sinners Christ died for us. (Romans 5:8)

With age-old love I have loved you;
    so I have kept my mercy toward you. (Jeremiah 31:3)

Highlight, underline, or bookmark any verses that stand out to you. You might want to journal about them.

CHAPTER SIX

Getting the "Most" Out of Adoration

A final question for many of us who struggle to mentally downshift during prayer or who really like practical steps is, how can I get more or the most out of my time in Adoration?

There are several tips I normally offer, based on my own successes and failures. Allow me to throw out a few simple ones here:

1. Bring your Bible. I don't suggest reading the entire time you are there, but sometimes his holy word allows us to center our hearts in a more focused and intentional way. In the following chapter, I'm going to offer you twelve Scripture reflections with some questions that will help you pray during Adoration. Now, these are just suggestions, meant to help you enter more deeply into his presence. They are not meant to fill your time so full that you don't have ample opportunity to listen to God.

2. Bring a journal or something to write in. You may not open or use this, but having it available will allow you to record thoughts or movements of the heart, without forgetting them or obsessing about them. You never know

when the Lord is going to speak, so having something to write on is important. You might prefer to take notes on your phone, but that can be distracting—to you(because of other notifications) and to other adorers. So a journal is optimal.

3. Silence your phone, and keep it in your pocket or purse. Or you might want to leave it in your car. We live in a noisy world in which we are always accessible. But if we are accessible to the world, our hearts cannot be fully accessible to God. Wear a watch if you are on the clock, and fight any temptation to look at your mobile device.

> **Go often to Holy Communion. Go very often! This is your one remedy.**
> **—St. Thérèse of Lisieux**

4. Know yourself. If you are easily distracted, sit close to the front. Pick your seat carefully, to avoid having your attention taken off the Lord. If kneeling for prolonged periods is difficult, kneel when you arrive and depart but sit comfortably while you adore. The Lord knows your physical limitations and thresholds. He would rather have your full attention and heart than ten more minutes on a kneeler.

5. If you flourish with structure and schedule, you can apply an internal "structure" to your Holy Hour (or holy half hour or holy fifteen minutes). For instance, if you plan to be in Adoration for an hour, try this:

- Spend the first five minutes exhaling and entering in. Leave behind traffic and tasks, and just breathe.
- Next, spend ten minutes giving thanks. Thank the Lord for all your blessings. Dig deep, offering gratitude for both the obvious and not so obvious blessings in your life.
- Then spend ten minutes in petition. Pray for all the people you are close to, have promised to pray for, and so on. Mention them by name: get them off your chest and into Christ's heart. Pray for situations that are weighing you down or stressing you out. Talk to the Lord, holding nothing back.
- Fourth, spend at least twenty-five minutes meditating on the Lord and what he may be saying to you. You can read Scripture and journal to help focus your prayer. This is really when you listen for what the Lord may be saying to you. Don't talk; just listen.
- Spend the last ten minutes or so in praise. Praise God for making himself available to you. Praise him for his goodness, his love, and his divine mercy. Even if you are suffering or struggling, pray a prayer of trust, such as "Lord, I don't always understand you, but I trust you." Pray it repeatedly if necessary. Over time you will find peace.

These steps, based on a Holy Hour, can be scaled down to fit into a holy half hour or even a holy fifteen minutes. Maybe you can stop at a chapel going to or from work or in between errands. The key is to make time to enter in and be heard and to really listen to what the Lord wants to speak to you.

CHAPTER SEVEN

Twelve Gospel Encounters for Adoration

Here are some Scripture passages that can act as prompts for prayerful thought, internal discussion, and discernment when you are in Adoration with our Lord.

ENCOUNTER ONE:
Jesus Calls Us to Love Our Enemies

Pray with Matthew 5:43–48.

"You have heard that it was said, 'You shall love your neighbor and hate your enemy.' But I say to you, love your enemies, and pray for those who persecute you, that you may be children of your heavenly Father, for he makes his sun rise on the bad and the good, and causes rain to fall on the just and the unjust. For if you love those who love you, what recompense will you have? Do not the tax collectors do the same? And if you greet your brothers only, what is unusual about that? Do not the pagans do the same? So be perfect, just as your heavenly Father is perfect."

Questions

1. How does one love an enemy?

2. Give an example of someone who showed you love when you didn't deserve it.

3. Is it possible to "be perfect, just as your heavenly Father is perfect"? What do you think Jesus meant by that statement?

Reflection

"But I say to you, love your enemies, and pray for those who persecute you" (Matthew 5:44). These are pretty tough words to swallow. Jesus speaks clearly, however, about his expectations for us.

It can be easy to love those who love us and treat us well, but it is hard to love those who hurt us. In your journal or on a sheet of paper, write the name(s) of person(s) in your life whom you find hard to love. Open to that page when you awake each morning, or tape the paper on your mirror so that you are reminded to pray for them.

Prayer

Your love is perfect, Jesus. Take my heart, and fill it with your perfect love. Teach me how to love and be patient with those who have treated me poorly, those I despise or find difficult to love. Amen.

ENCOUNTER TWO:
Jesus Delivers Us from Our Fear

Pray with Matthew 8:23-27.

He got into a boat and his disciples followed him. Suddenly a violent storm came up on the sea, so that the boat was being swamped by waves; but he was asleep. They came and woke him, saying, "Lord, save us! We are perishing!" He said to them, "Why are you terrified, O you of little faith?" Then he got up, rebuked the winds and the sea, and there was great calm. The men were amazed and said, "What sort of man is this, whom even the winds and the sea obey?"

> Jesus in the Blessed Sacrament is the Living Heart of each of our parishes.
> —Pope St. Paul VI

Questions

1. Is your faith strong enough to survive the storms of life?

2. What storms are you experiencing at this moment? Has God helped you through some of these storms in the past? If so, how?

3. Do you rely on God in times of fear?

Reflection

It's okay to worry, to be scared, and to feel fearful. It doesn't make you horrible; it makes you human. But it's important to remember that fear is not from God. "For God did not give us a spirit of cowardice but rather of power and love and self-control" (2 Timothy 1:7).

Fear has a tendency to take hold of us and consume us. If we constantly live in fear about things in our lives, we will not be able to truly live as Christ wants us to. Many of us worry about losing a loved one or losing a job or having health problems, all beyond our control. We worry about the future, being lonely, being successful, or being a failure.

It is normal to think about these things, but when fear begins to take over, it can render us unable to move forward in faith and peace. Only Jesus can calm the storms and fears in our lives.

What is your biggest fear? Name it as you kneel before Jesus in the Eucharist. Allow God to give you the courage you need to face your fears.

Prayer

Jesus, help me see you and hear you clearly amid the storms in my life, that I may not be afraid of anything. I put my trust in you. You alone are my Savior. Deliver me from fear, and grant me the courage to follow you daily. Amen.

ENCOUNTER THREE:
Jesus Delivers Us from Doubt

Pray with Matthew 16:15-20.

[Jesus] said to them, "But who do you say that I am?" Simon Peter said in reply, "You are the Messiah, the Son of the living God." Jesus said to him in reply, "Blessed are you, Simon son of Jonah. For flesh and blood has not revealed this to you, but my heavenly Father. And so I say to you, you are Peter, and upon this rock I will build my church, and the gates of the netherworld shall not prevail against it. I will give you the keys to the kingdom of heaven. Whatever you bind on earth shall be bound in heaven; and whatever you loose on earth shall be loosed in heaven." Then he strictly ordered his disciples to tell no one that he was the Messiah.

Questions

1. Did you ever doubt that Jesus is truly the "Son of the living God," our Savior? Why did you doubt?

2. What can you do to lessen any doubts you have?

3. Is having doubts about who God is always bad? Why or why not?

Reflection

Who do you say Jesus is? Do you truly believe he is the Messiah? There are times in our lives when we question our belief in God. Even Peter, our first pope, denied Jesus. Peter recognized his weakness, however, and pursued the Lord with renewed vigor.

It's okay to be doubtful. If you haven't doubted from time to time, that might be a cause for concern. Have you really thought about your faith and its implications?

Turn any doubt into an opportunity. Pursue Jesus with an open heart.

Write out the areas or topics that cause your trust to waver and your doubts to mount. Bring them to the Lord in Adoration. Be honest and transparent in your prayer. He already knows the movements of your mind and heart. Trust that he will answer you and speak to those movements in due time.

> Through adoration the Christian mysteriously contributes to the radical transformation of the world and to the sowing of the gospel. Anyone who prays to the Eucharistic Savior draws the whole world with him and raises it to God.
> —Pope St. John Paul II

Prayer

Jesus, deliver me from doubting you and your love. Give me the eyes to see you working in my life. Give me a heart that is open to your truth, and lead me into a deeper faith in you. Amen.

ENCOUNTER FOUR:
Jesus Delivers Us from Our Demons

Pray with Mark 5:1-13.

They came to the other side of the sea, to the territory of the Gerasenes. When he got out of the boat, at once a man from the tombs who had an unclean spirit met him. The man had been dwelling among the tombs, and no one could restrain him any longer, even with a chain. In fact, he had frequently been bound with shackles and chains, but the chains had been pulled apart by him and the shackles smashed, and no one was strong enough to subdue him. Night and day among the tombs and on the hillsides he was always crying out and bruising himself with stones. Catching sight of Jesus from a distance, he ran up and prostrated himself before him, crying out in a loud voice, "What have you to do with me, Jesus, Son of the Most High God? I adjure you by God, do not torment me!" (He had been saying to him, "Unclean spirit, come out of the man!") He asked him, "What is your name?" He replied, "Legion is my name. There are many of us." And he pleaded earnestly with him not to drive them away from that territory.

Now a large herd of swine was feeding there on the hillside. And they pleaded with him, "Send us into the swine. Let us enter them." And he let them, and the unclean spirits came out and entered the swine. The herd of about two thousand rushed down a steep bank into the sea, where they were drowned.

Questions

1. Do you see yourself as generally good or bad? Why?

2. Do you believe God is more powerful than the evil in the world? Why or why not?

3. What can you do in your daily life to keep evil away?

Reflection

It says in Philippians 2:10-11 that "every knee should bend, . . . and every tongue confess that Jesus Christ is Lord." Jesus himself is our greatest strength but, too often, the last one to whom we go. We try to defeat the demons in our lives on our own, failing to realize that it cannot be done. We are totally helpless and outmatched. Jesus has healing power and authority over all things, and only with Jesus can we overcome the demons in our lives.

Do you have struggles? Are there things in your life you can't overcome? Are you weighed down by sin?

Ask Jesus for help. He will always be there.

> Do not think that Jesus Christ is forgetful of you, since he has left you, as the greatest memorial and pledge of his love, himself in the Most Holy Sacrament of the Altar.
> —St. Alphonsus Liguori

Prayer

Lord, I have made every attempt at breaking these chains that bind me. Now I realize that I cannot be free on my own. Powerful God, deliver me from the demons in my life. Break these chains, Lord, so that I may be free to live in your love. Amen.

ENCOUNTER FIVE:
Jesus Reminds Us to Take Time to Pray

Pray with Mark 6:30-32.

> The apostles gathered together with Jesus and reported all they had done and taught. He said to them, "Come away by yourselves to a deserted place and rest a while." People were coming and going in great numbers, and they had no opportunity even to eat. So they went off in the boat by themselves to a deserted place.

Questions

1. What is the purpose of prayer in your life?

2. Why did Jesus have the apostles go off by themselves to pray?

3. Is prayer a priority in your daily life? Why or why not?

Reflection

When do you pray? Do you only pray when you need something or when things are going wrong and stress has taken over?

Prayer is not solely about asking for things; it's about communicating with Jesus on a regular basis. It is an ascent of our minds and hearts to God. Prayer is our lifeline; it is where the cross changes shoulders.

We need to get into a daily rhythm. Whether it be five minutes or thirty, we need to take time daily to be with Jesus. So take a hard look at how you set up your day and life. Be honest with yourself about the role prayer has played of late.

Prayer

Thank you, Jesus, for the gift of prayer. Create in me the desire to pray more. Help me take time to listen for your voice, to praise you for what you've done for me, to ask for your help, and to pray for others in need of your love. Amen.

ENCOUNTER SIX:
Serve the Lord

Pray with Mark 10:43–45.

"[W]hoever wishes to be great among you will be your servant; whoever wishes to be first among you will be the slave of all. For the Son of Man did not come to be served but to serve and to give his life as a ransom for many."

Questions

1. Do you view your daily tasks as service of the Lord? Why or why not?

2. St. Teresa of Calcutta reminded us, "In this life we cannot do great things. We can only do small things with great love." What are some small things that can become acts of love in your household, your family, or your community?

3. How is God calling you to serve in your neighborhood, home, or parish?

Reflection

Jesus came not to be served but to serve. How do we practice this?

There is a crucial difference between serving others for the sake of getting a job done and serving others out of love. We are called to serve others not just when it suits us but also when it's a true sacrifice. Selfless love, serving until it hurts, is a lesson we learn from and at the cross of Christ.

Think of the way a parent cares for their newborn baby: night after night of little sleep, possible headache from the child's restless crying, sheer exhaustion. This kind of self-sacrificing, love-fueled service is what Christ calls us to.

There are many types of service. Ours doesn't have to be a huge act; little things, the seemingly mundane, are often the most difficult. The important thing is to look at where your heart is. Are you serving as Christ would, out of love?

> When the Sisters are exhausted, up to their eyes in work; when all seems to go awry, they spend an hour in prayer before the Blessed Sacrament. This practice has never failed to bear fruit: they experience peace and strength.
> —St. Teresa of Calcutta

Go out of your way to serve someone today without seeking recognition or thanks.

Prayer

Jesus, help me want to serve you every day. Help me see your face in those around me, and know that, by serving them with love, I am serving you. Help me recognize that with your help, I can do small things with great love. Amen.

ENCOUNTER SEVEN:
Jesus Delivers Us from Pain

Pray with Luke 8:43-48.

A woman afflicted with hemorrhages for twelve years, who [had spent her whole livelihood on doctors and] was unable to be cured by anyone, came up behind him and touched the tassel on his cloak. Immediately her bleeding stopped. Jesus then asked, "Who touched me?" While all were denying it, Peter said, "Master, the crowds are pushing and pressing in upon you." But Jesus said, "Someone has touched me; for I know that power has gone out from me." When the woman realized that she had not escaped notice, she came forward trembling. Falling down before him, she explained in the presence of all the people why she had touched him and how she had been healed immediately. He said to her, "Daughter, your faith has saved you; go in peace."

Questions

1. Do you or does someone you know suffer from physical, emotional, or spiritual pain? How has this suffering impacted your faith in God?

2. In what ways does God heal our hurts today?

3. Have you experienced the healing touch of God in your life? If so, how?

Reflection

Ask yourself this question: "Can God heal my pain?" Note that this is a different question from "Will you heal my pain now, God?" We better believe he can, but we have to trust not only in God's power but also in his providential timing.

Jesus didn't perform miracles just back then; he also performs them today. What kind of pain do you have in your life? Do you have some deep hurts or wounds from the past?

Be open and honest with God about your pain. Give him time, and put your trust in him.

Prayer

Heal me, Jesus. Heal my heart if it is broken, my soul if it is weary, and my faith if it is weak. Deliver me from my pain, and bring me into the same joy that was felt by those you have healed throughout time. Amen.

ENCOUNTER EIGHT:
Jesus Faced Temptation

Pray with Luke 4:1-13.

Filled with the holy Spirit, Jesus returned from the Jordan and was led by the Spirit into the desert for forty days, to be tempted by the devil. He ate nothing during those days, and when they were over he was hungry. The devil said to him, "If you are the Son of God, command this stone to become bread." Jesus answered him, "It is written, 'One does not live by bread alone.'" Then he took him up and showed him all the kingdoms of the world in a single instant. The devil said to him, "I shall give to you all this power and their glory; for it has been handed over to me, and I may give it to whomever I wish. All this will be yours, if you worship me." Jesus said to him in reply, "It is written:

'You shall worship the Lord, your God,
    and him alone shall you serve.'"

Then he led him to Jerusalem, made him stand on the parapet of the temple, and said to him, "If you are the Son of God, throw yourself down from here, for it is written:

'He will command his angels concerning you,
    to guard you,'

and:

'With their hands they will support you,
    lest you dash your foot against a stone.'"

Jesus said to him in reply, "It also says, 'You shall not put the Lord, your God, to the test.'" When the devil had finished every temptation, he departed from him for a time.

Questions

1. Do you have a hard time fighting temptation? What temptation do you struggle with the most?

2. Temptation leads to sin. How does God help us fight the temptations the devil throws before us?

3. The Scripture passage says, "And when the devil had ended every temptation, he departed from him until an opportune time" (Luke 4:13, RSVCE). What does that mean?

Reflection

Jesus was tempted just as we are, and he resisted temptation; he never gave in to Satan's antics. Jesus is our model. We can resist any temptation with God's help.

St. Paul tells us that we can accomplish all things through Christ (see Philippians 4:13). Today, turn your back on temptation. Set boundaries, and don't be afraid to say no to the evil one.

> A thousand years of enjoying human glory is not worth even an hour spent sweetly communing with Jesus in the Blessed Sacrament.
> —St. Pio of Pietrelcina

Prayer

Be with me, Jesus. In my times of temptation, hold me in your grace. Give me the strength to turn to you.

I cannot avoid sin on my own, Lord; I am weak. But in your love, I am strong.

In the name of Jesus, I rebuke the evil one. Amen.

ENCOUNTER NINE:
Jesus Remains with Us in the Eucharist

Pray with Luke 24:13-32.

Now that very day two of them were going to a village seven miles from Jerusalem called Emmaus, and they were conversing about all the things that had occurred. And it happened that while they were conversing and debating, Jesus himself drew near and walked with them, but their eyes were prevented from recognizing him. He asked them, "What are you discussing as you walk along?" They stopped, looking downcast. One of them, named Cleopas, said to him in reply, "Are you the only visitor to Jerusalem who does not know of the things that have taken place there in these days?" And he replied to them, "What sort of things?" They said to him, "The things that happened to Jesus the Nazarene, who was a prophet mighty in deed and word before God and all the people, how our chief priests and rulers both handed him over to a sentence of death and crucified him. But we were hoping that he would be the one to redeem Israel; and besides all this, it is now the third day since this took place. Some women from our group, however, have astounded us: they were at the tomb early in the morning and did not find his body; they came back and reported that they had indeed seen a vision of angels who announced that he was alive. Then some of those with us went to the tomb and found things just as the women had described, but him they did not see." And he said to them, "Oh, how foolish you are! How slow of heart to believe all that the prophets spoke! Was it not necessary that the Messiah should suffer these things and enter into his glory?" Then beginning with Moses and all the prophets, he interpreted to them what referred to him in all the scriptures. As they approached the village to which they were going, he gave the impression that he was going on farther. But they urged him, "Stay with us, for it is nearly evening and the day is almost over." So he went in to stay with them. And it happened that, while he was with them at table, he took bread, said the blessing, broke it, and gave it to them. With that their eyes were opened and they recognized him, but he vanished from their sight. Then they said to each other, "Were not our hearts burning [within us] while he spoke to us on the way and opened the scriptures to us?"

> I have nothing more to tell you. You already have the Eucharist. What more do you want?
> —St. Peter Julian Eymard

Questions

1. Are you willing to allow Christ to be part of your life and to change it? If not, why not? If so, how?

2. The lives of Jesus' apostles were changed following his death and resurrection. How has Jesus' resurrection affected your life?

3. Do you believe Jesus is truly present in the Eucharist? Why or why not?

Reflection

This passage, recording an event after Jesus rose from the grave, is one of the most amazing passages in all of Scripture. The disciples were not expecting the Lord to reveal himself as he did. If this passage teaches us anything, it's that the Lord can be right in front of us, and we may not recognize him (as is the case with the Eucharist).

Notice that Jesus first entered into the disciples' presence and suffering and asked them questions. He wanted to know what they were feeling. He then offered wisdom and insight and perspective, which brought them peace to a point where their hearts were "burning" within them. All the while, Jesus was walking with them and leading them straight to the altar.

When the Lord broke the bread, the disciples realized it was he. They were left staring upon the Eucharist as Jesus vanished from their sight. Stop and ponder this reality in Adoration, and really let it sink in.

Prayer

Thank you, Jesus. You are the Messiah, the Son of the living God. You are the King of all kings, the only true God.

Thank you for the gift of the Eucharist. Give me eyes of faith, that I may come to know and experience the depths of your love

> It would be easier for the world to survive without the sun than to do so without the Holy Mass.
> —St. Pio of Pietrelcina

made available through your Body and Blood. Give me a new respect and reverence for the Eucharist. Quiet my mind and heart when I am at Mass and Adoration so that I may begin to understand the incredible mystery of the Eucharist. Amen.

ENCOUNTER TEN:
Jesus Shows Us Compassion

Pray with John 8:2-11.

[E]arly in the morning [Jesus] arrived again in the temple area, and all the people started coming to him, and he sat down and taught them. Then the scribes and the Pharisees brought a woman who had been caught in adultery and made her stand in the middle. They said to him, "Teacher, this woman was caught in the very act of committing adultery. Now in the law, Moses commanded us to stone such women. So what do you say?" They said this to test him, so that they could have some charge to bring against him. Jesus bent down and began to write on the ground with his finger. But when they continued asking him, he straightened up and said to them, "Let the one among you who is without sin be the first to throw a stone at her." Again he bent down and wrote on the ground. And in response, they went away one by one, beginning with the elders. So he was left alone with the woman before him. Then Jesus straightened up and said to her, "Woman, where are they? Has no one condemned you?" She replied, "No one, sir." Then Jesus said, "Neither do I condemn you. Go, [and] from now on do not sin any more."

Questions

1. When you sin, who do you think condemns you: your friends, your family, yourself, or God?

2. Are you hesitant or afraid to go to the Sacrament of Reconciliation? Why or why not?

3. Have you ever reflected on your own sinful ways after you judged someone else for theirs? What was that experience like?

Reflection

This Scripture passage offers us two challenges: to forgive and not to judge. Both are tough to practice, but they are what Jesus calls us to do and not to do.

Is there someone in your life whom you have judged? Do you have the courage to approach that person (if it is appropriate) and ask forgiveness?

Is there someone in your life who has judged you or whom you need to forgive? Are you willing to forgive them?

Prayer

Jesus, help me see my own sin before noticing the sins of others. Show me your compassion, Lord, and take away any fear I have of the Sacrament of Reconciliation. Make me receptive to your mercy, Jesus. Amen.

ENCOUNTER ELEVEN:
Jesus Delivers Us from Death

Pray with John 11:30–44.

Jesus had not yet come into the village [where Lazarus had lived] . . . . So when the Jews who were with [Mary] in the house comforting her saw Mary get up quickly and go out, they followed her, presuming that she was going to the tomb to weep there. When Mary came to where Jesus was and saw him, she fell at his feet and said to him, "Lord, if you had been here, my brother would not have died." When Jesus saw her weeping and the Jews who had come with her weeping, he became perturbed and deeply troubled, and said, "Where have you laid him?" They said to him, "Sir, come and see." And Jesus wept. So the Jews said, "See how he loved him." But some of them said, "Could not the one who opened the eyes of the blind man have done something so that this man would not have died?"

So Jesus, perturbed again, came to the tomb. It was a cave, and a stone lay across it. Jesus said, "Take away the stone." Martha, the dead man's sister, said to him, "Lord, by now there will be a stench; he has been dead for four days." Jesus said to her, "Did I not tell you that if you believe you will see the glory of God?" So they took away the stone. And Jesus raised his eyes and said, "Father, I thank you for hearing me. I know that you always hear me; but because of the crowd here I have said this, that they may believe that you sent me." And when he had said this, he cried out in a loud voice, "Lazarus, come out!" The dead man came out, tied hand and foot with burial bands, and his face was wrapped in a cloth. So Jesus said to them, "Untie him and let him go."

Questions

1. "Jesus wept" (John 11:35). Do you see God as a compassionate God? Why or why not?

2. Why did Jesus raise Lazarus from the dead?

3. Do you believe God can transform your life? If so, in what parts of your life would you like to see him work?

Reflection

Does death scare you? It is our hope as sons and daughters of God that, when we die, we will share eternal life with Jesus and the saints. The catch is that we can't be spiritually dead here on earth. Jesus reminds us that he is the answer to both physical and spiritual death. He is calling us, as he called Lazarus, out of the tomb.

Are you dead in your faith? Is your spiritual life nonexistent or struggling?

Jesus is calling you out of the tomb to experience a new life in him. Wake up, come out, and embrace life. Give someone a smile or a hug today. And when you do, remind yourself of the importance of living each day to the fullest.

Prayer

Thank you, Lord, for the gift of life. Give me the grace to live for you completely. Awaken my heart if it is numb or dead; fill it with faith and passion for you. Amen.

ENCOUNTER TWELVE:
Jesus Calls Us to Serve One Another

Pray with John 13:3-9.

[F]ully aware that the Father had put everything into his power and that he had come from God and was returning to God, he rose from supper and took off his outer garments. He took a towel and tied it around his waist. Then he poured water into a basin and began to wash the disciples' feet and dry them with the towel around his waist. He came to Simon Peter, who said to him, "Master, are you going to wash my feet?" Jesus answered and said to him, "What I am doing, you do not understand now, but you will understand later." Peter said to him, "You will never wash my feet." Jesus answered him, "Unless I wash you, you will have no inheritance with me." Simon Peter said to him, "Master, then not only my feet, but my hands and head as well."

Questions

1. Do you see yourself as a foot washer (serving) or more as someone who has your feet washed (being served)?

2. Give two examples of "foot washers" who have affected your life.

3. In what ways can you be a foot washer to others?

Reflection

There are innumerable ways in which Jesus could have spent his final hours with his closest followers. Why would Jesus choose to wash the feet of the disciples?

"The Son of Man did not come to be served but to serve" (Matthew 20:28; Mark 10:45). Jesus knew serving God meant serving others.

Serving can be tough: it means putting others' needs before our own. Think of something tangible you can do this week for others. Make time to help someone in need. Clean out a closet, and donate items to the Society of Saint Vincent de Paul. Offer to help a neighbor. Clean the house. Do laundry. There are a thousand sacrifices that may seem small on earth but cause heaven to applaud.

Prayer

Lord God, you created everything. You came to this earth in human form to serve. Change my heart into that of a servant's heart. May I do good for others and expect nothing in return.

When my pride gets in the way, Lord, remind me of how you washed your disciples' feet and served those in need. Nothing is beyond you. Thank you, Jesus. Amen.

Do you want the Lord to give you many graces? Visit Him often. Do you want Him to give you few graces? Visit Him rarely. Do you want the devil to attack you? Visit Jesus rarely in the Blessed Sacrament. Do you want him to flee from you? Visit Jesus often. Do you want to conquer the devil? Take refuge often at the feet of Jesus. Do you want to be conquered by the devil? Forget about visiting Jesus. My dear ones, the visit to the Blessed Sacrament is an extremely necessary way to conquer the devil. Therefore, go often to visit Jesus and the devil will not come out victorious against you.
—St. John Bosco

Appendix

What Is Benediction?

For those times when Adoration takes place before the exposed Eucharist (and not before the reserved Eucharist in the tabernacle), Benediction may celebrated at the conclusion of the exposition, as the Eucharist is reposed in the tabernacle. In this moment, we receive God's grace in a special way. Benediction is the blessing of Jesus in the Blessed Sacrament, which makes it unique. The Church teaches that this blessing is meant to give grace and also help us return to Christ in the Eucharist—in Adoration and, more importantly, in the celebration of the Mass.

When the priest or deacon begins Benediction, the people kneel in preparation for the blessing. The priest or deacon usually wears a *humeral veil,* which he uses to cover his hands when he picks up the monstrance and offers the blessing. He wears this veil both to show respect for the monstrance, which shows the Eucharist to the people, and as a sign that it is not he who gives the blessing but Jesus Christ himself.

Hymns and Prayers for Benediction

Tantum Ergo

Tantum ergo Sacramentum
Veneremur cernui:
Et antiquum documentum
Novo cedat ritui:
Praestet fides supplementum
Sensuum defectui.

Genitori, Genitoque,
Laus et iubilatio,
Salus, honor, virtus quoque
Sit et benedictio:
Procedenti ab utroque
Compar sit laudatio. Amen.

V. Panem de caelo praestitisti eis.
R. Omne delectamentum in se habentem.
V. Oremus: Deus, qui nobis sub sacramento mirabili, passionis tuae memoriam reliquisti: tribue, quaesumus, ita nos corporis et sanguinis tui sacra mysteria venerari, ut redemptionis tuae fructum in nobis iugiter sentiamus. Qui vivis et regnas in saecula saeculorum.
R. Amen.

Down in Adoration Falling (Tantum Ergo in English)

Down in adoration falling,
Lo! the sacred Host we hail.
Lo! O'er ancient forms departing
Newer rites of grace prevail;
Faith for all defects supplying,
Where the feeble senses fail.

To the everlasting Father,
And the Son who reigns on high
With the Holy Spirit proceeding
Forth from each eternally,
Be salvation, honor, blessing,
Might and endless majesty.
Amen.

V. Thou hast given them bread from heaven.
R. Having within it all sweetness.
V. Let us pray: O God, who in this wonderful Sacrament left
us a memorial of thy passion, grant, we implore thee, that
we may so venerate the sacred mysteries of thy Body and
Blood, as always to be conscious of the fruit of thy redemp-
tion. Thou who livest and reignest forever and ever.
R. Amen.

The Divine Praises (often offered in a call-and-response manner)

Blessed be God.
Blessed be his Holy Name.
Blessed be Jesus Christ, true God and true man.
Blessed be the name of Jesus.
Blessed be his Most Sacred Heart.
Blessed be his Most Precious Blood.
Blessed be Jesus in the Most Holy Sacrament of the Altar.
Blessed be the Holy Spirit, the Paraclete.
Blessed be the great Mother of God, Mary Most Holy.
Blessed be her Holy and Immaculate Conception.
Blessed be her Glorious Assumption.
Blessed be the name of Mary, Virgin and Mother.
Blessed be St. Joseph, her most chaste spouse.
Blessed be God in his Angels and in his Saints.

The St. Michael Prayer

St. Michael the Archangel, defend us in battle.
Be our protection against the wickedness and snares of
the devil.
May God rebuke him, we humbly pray.
And do thou, O prince of the heavenly host, by the power
of God,
cast into hell Satan and all evil spirits
who prowl about the world seeking the ruin of souls. Amen.

About the Author

Mark Hart is affectionately known to millions across the world as the Bible Geek. Mark is a bestselling author of numerous books, including *Behold the Mystery: A Deeper Understanding of the Catholic Mass*. He is also a highly sought-after speaker and radio personality. Mark serves as the Chief Innovation Officer of Life Teen International. Mark and his wife, Melanie, have four children and live in Phoenix, Arizona.

Books by Mark Hart

Behold the Mystery: A Deeper Understanding of the Catholic Mass
Mark Hart helps Catholics see the Mass for what it really is: a heavenly banquet, a wedding feast, in which heaven and earth meet. In his engaging style, Hart guides readers toward a deeper understanding of the Mass—its roots in the Jewish Sabbath, its sacrificial character, and its signs and symbols.
Product Code: BMORE3

Embracing God's Plan for Marriage
Marriage is one of God's most beautiful gifts and is intended to bless us, fulfill us, and give us a path to sanctity. Understanding what true love entails and how grace works to overcome our wounded human nature is the key to a holy, happy, and passionate marriage. In this six-session Bible study, popular author and speaker Mark Hart and his wife, Melanie, help couples understand key Scripture passages that illuminate the truths about married love.
Product Code: BGPME2

Unleashing the Power of Scripture

In his entertaining and engaging style, Mark Hart shows readers why Scripture should be central to our lives. When we become immersed in Scripture, we allow it to form our minds and hearts. This book also considers the place of Scripture in the liturgy, the practice of *lectio divina*, the prayerful reading of Scripture, and shows how the Scriptures connect to the sacraments. Includes a step-by-step plan to establish the habit of reading Scripture.
Product Code: BLCPE4

Getting More Out of Mass

In the liturgy of the Mass, life-giving power flows from the body of Jesus. This booklet will help you become more receptive to the abundant life and healing love that God wants to give you each week. Discover a fresh lens for truly understanding each part of the Mass—as well as practical advice for staying prayerful and focused.
Product Code: BHMSE8

Getting More Out of the Eucharist

The Catechism tells us the Eucharist is the "source and summit" of our faith. So coming to understand, both intellectually and spiritually, the amazing gift that Jesus left to his Church will transform your life. Learn how Jesus comes to us, giving us his real flesh and his real blood, to console us and strengthen us for our walk as his followers.
Product Code: BHEUE9